Newness of Life:
Trusting God in Times of Transition

by Sarah Geringer

For Dawn
The encouraging friend God handpicked for me
at the perfect time

Acknowledgments

Thanks to many who have read my first e-book, *Christmas Peace for Busy Moms*. You have encouraged me to keep writing more books for readers yet unknown!

Thanks to my husband and children for your patience, support, and understanding as I traded many hours of family time for writing time.

Thanks to family members who took care of our children so I could immerse myself in writing this book over Christmas break.

Thanks to Angie, who provided fresh ideas on how to develop several chapters. God sent your insight to me at just the right time, dear friend!

Thanks to my launch team members. I appreciate your reading this in such a short time span. May God bless you with newness of life.

Thanks to Michael Hyatt, Jeff Goins, Tim Grahl, Chandler Bolt, and Sarah Mae for your online training and e-books which have powerfully shaped my writing career. I haven't met you yet, but I count you as my mentors.

Above all, thanks go to my Lord and Savior, Jesus Christ, the One who deserves all the glory. I want my seasons, times, and activities to point others to you.

Table of Contents

Welcome to Newness of Life

Anyone who belongs to Christ has become a new person. The old life is gone; a new life has begun! 2 Corinthians 5:17 NLT

Are you searching for newness of life in your current season?

Perhaps you are in a season of pain: tearing down, grieving, letting go.

Perhaps you are in a season of recovery: mending, gathering, healing.

Perhaps you are in a season of joy: building up, planting, dancing.

No matter what season you are in today, God's timing is perfect. He is creating new life for you now. New peace, new joy, and new hope perfectly tailored for this time in your life.

How is your faith staying true in the changes? Can you really trust God in your current season and seasons to come? That's what this study is about. It's applying the scriptures in Ecclesiastes 3:1-8 so you can understand God's plan in different seasons.

All you need for this study is a Bible, a notebook, and your favorite pen. Visit **www.sarahgeringer.com/freebies** for exclusive, additional Newness of Life resources and access to my library of free materials.

My times are in your hands. Psalm 31:15

God is holding you in his hand in this special time. This study will help you discover what God is teaching you about your current season, and what newness of life is available to you.

I am grateful you are here with me. Let's begin this journey of trusting in God's perfect timing.

Chapter 1: Life's Seasons

For everything there is a season.
Ecclesiastes 3:1 NLT

What is your favorite season?

I am blessed to live in a temperate climate, where I experience all four seasons. Spring's floral parade. Summer's green bounty. Autumn's glorious color. Winter's stark beauty.

Of all the seasons, fall is my favorite. I'm an October baby and I love all things pumpkin. I adore cozy sweaters, crisp mornings, and bonfires. The scent of drying leaves captivates me as I walk through our wooded property.

As I write this book, December is drawing to a close and January soon approaches. I am saying goodbye to this beloved season of lights, decor, cookies, concerts, and family time. I am greeting the new year with hope, anticipation, and gratitude.

What feelings are swirling in your current season of life?

Years ago I listened to the late Jean Lush on a Focus on the Family broadcast. Her intelligence and wit drew me in. Thanks to the availability of used books online, I ordered several of her titles and drank from the wells of her godly wisdom. Her book *Emotional Phases of a Woman's Life* taught me much about the physical and emotional season I am in.

Now in the "summer" phase of life, I often feel as if I'm running in high gear, even sometimes in survival mode, like I do when tending my garden in mid-July. My three children are old enough to manage themselves yet still need much attention. They are growing like weeds, seemingly overnight! We will enter the exciting and challenging teen years in a few months.

My husband and I are both working hard. We are blessed with much, not mired in debt the way we used to be, but extra dollars are hard to come by. This season is financially challenging and I feel way behind on saving for the future.

Our schedules are packed with activities on evenings and weekends. Much effort is required to maintain connections simply in our own home, much less with extended family and friends.

And pursuing my dream to write is requiring much time, energy, and effort. Yet I've put my dreams on hold so long, I can't push them back down any longer. Even if I must write in the early mornings before work and log extra time on the weekends, writing fulfills me like nothing else.

As challenging as this season feels, I love this season with our children still at home. I seek wisdom from those who have faced this summer season before, so I can face what's ahead with faith.

In this book I will share about past seasons I've experienced, in the hope you will be encouraged to face your next season with faith.

Will you also share how your faith has grown through past seasons? Join in the discussion at the Newness of Life Facebook group.

Are you arguing with God over whether this season is right for you, or are you satisfied? Are you frightened? Are you uncertain?

I remember certain thresholds and the feelings of excitement, anxiety, and hope...

At thirteen I was a newly confirmed Lutheran, salutatorian of my eighth grade class, afraid of boys, curious about boys, excited about high school, in love with Harry Connick Jr. and INXS.

At twenty-three I was a newlywed, art student with an English degree, afraid of abandonment, curious about homemaking, excited about getting a real job, in love with romance.

At thirty-three I was a new fan of counseling, mother of three young children, afraid of divorce, curious about blogging, excited about building mommy friendships, in love with naps.

At today's threshold, what is new for you?

What is your main title?
What is your biggest fear?
What makes you curious?
What gets you excited?
What stirs your love?

Friend, as we begin this journey together, remember God has ordained each season of your life. He is guiding you through and can't wait to teach you new things, custom-made for the season you're in.

In the season of thirteen, He gave me a love for his Word.
In the season of twenty-three, He taught me about forgiveness.
In the season of thirty-three, He showed me how to set boundaries.

What is He teaching you now, new for this season?

For everything there is a season. Whatever season you face now, God is in it with you. Through this study we will learn how to trust him inside these unique seasons, in all the times necessary for spiritual growth.

Keep this verse in mind:

Being confident of this, that he who began a good work in you will carry it on to completion until the day of Christ Jesus. Philippians 1:6

The change God sparks in you now is intended to make you more like Jesus. The challenges will shape your character, and your experiences can be used to bless others coming behind you.

Prayer:

Heavenly Father,
I want to trust in your perfect timing. I want to learn from others who have already gone through my current season, and I want to help others now experiencing seasons I've already known. Help me reflect on what you have taught me in the past. Show me what lessons you want me to learn in this current season. Give me a spirit of confidence in you for the future.
In Jesus' name, Amen.

Questions for Study and Reflection:

Read Psalm 1:3. How has God cultivated you to bear fruit in season this year?

When have you experienced a season of singing, as described in Song of Songs 2:12?

Pick three life thresholds. What did God teach you in each of those seasons?

Read Daniel 2:21. What does this verse teach you about God's sovereignty (his perfect, transcendent rule over all things)?

Look up Ezekiel 34:26. What showers of blessing might God have in store for you in your current season?

Chapter 2: Birth and Death

A time to be born and a time to die.
Ecclesiastes 3:2

Have you ever felt out-of-place in the time period to which you were born?

If I could pick any time period, it would be the late 1800's here in the Midwest, in the time Laura Ingalls Wilder described in her Little House on the Prairie books. I fell in love with these books as a child. They reminded me of simpler times my great-grandma described in her childhood stories.

But my great-grandma often warned me, "Don't long for the old days. They were so much work." She was well into her sixties before she had any modern conveniences. Her hands were worn from years of hard work on the family farm. I have to admit, I would feel lost without indoor plumbing and my dishwasher.

If I count my household machines, I have over a dozen helpers assisting me in my daily life, ones my great-grandma and Laura Ingalls Wilder didn't have. My helpers wash dishes, wash clothing and linens, sweep floors, "tote" water, heat our home and water supply, cool and preserve food, prepare our food without a hearth, keep lamps lit, provide entertainment and transportation, and help me write and communicate more efficiently. Have you ever considered how many helpers you have in the time God has placed you?

I was born into the Information Age as a Generation X baby. As overwhelming as it can be to keep up with new technology and the wealth of available content, I thank God for placing me in this time period. I can write and blog online and develop a following before I am ever recognized by a traditional publisher. That wasn't possible when I graduated from college in 2001—not so long ago.

Possibilities abound in this Information Age. Yet, do you ever feel like you want to run and hide from all the possibilities? Do you still face nagging doubt that this fast-paced time period, this particular season, is right for you?

There are days when I face doubts and fears that all my effort won't lead to dream fulfillment. There are mornings when I rise early to write and a quiet doubt whispers, *Will this forever be an expensive hobby? Will I have anything to show for all my time? Does it really matter?*

When I doubt God's timing, I consider Joseph's story in the book of Genesis. Favored by his father but despised and rejected by his brothers, Joseph was sold into slavery as a young man. He was falsely accused of misconduct and thrown into prison. There he sat for years in darkness, surely considering the dream God gave him as a teen, as he had (perhaps unwisely) shared with his brothers:

Listen to this dream I had: We were binding sheaves of grain out in the field when suddenly my sheaf rose and stood upright, while your sheaves gathered around mine and bowed down to it. Genesis 37:6-7

I wonder if the question Joseph asked God most often was not *Why?,* but *When?*

When will I be set free for doing nothing wrong?
When will I see my beloved father and baby brother again?
When will I rise above this, as you promised, Lord?

Joseph's story is a marvelous example of God's perfect timing. After years in prison, Joseph miraculously interpreted a dream for Pharoah, and he was crowned second-in-charge over all Egypt, the most powerful empire at that time. When a devastating famine struck, Joseph's family came to Egypt for grain. Joseph recognized them, reconciled with them, and brought them to Egypt. God's people survived a world famine because Joseph rose to power at exactly the right time.

Joseph acknowledged his trust in God's timing when his brothers were afraid he may kill them:

You intended to harm me, but God intended it for good to accomplish what is now being done, the saving of many lives. Genesis 50:20

I doubt Joseph understood God's timing while he sat in prison. Many of us have faced seasons of obscurity when God's timing is difficult to understand or makes no sense at all.
What if Joseph had given up? What if he had not tried to interpret the dream? What if his faith had failed in prison, and he no longer believed the dream God gave him?

God's people would have suffered. The body of believers would have missed out on much blessing.

My *time to be born* is not only about me. It's about affecting others for good in the time I'm here.

Of course, none of us knows when our *time to die* will arrive. Only God knows, and He doesn't reveal it so I will work hard for his kingdom as long as I'm here.

My favorite movie as a teen was *Dead Poets' Society*. The movie's theme is *carpe diem*, which means "seize the day" in Latin. As a teen I decided to live intentionally, making every day count for something. My deep desire then was to have my life count, to leave fingerprints on every aspect of my life.

To be someone people didn't forget.

Perhaps because I often felt forgotten, like Joseph in prison.

In my *time to be born*, God never forgot me. My name is written on the palms of his hands (Is. 49:16 NLT). My days were written in his book *before* I was born (Ps. 139: 16). My name is written in his book of life (Rev. 21:27). He has never forgotten me and never will, and He has plans for me which are good and trustworthy (Jer. 29:11). He has plans for me to help others in the world and in the great body of believers. He will hold me in His hand until that unknown day when it is my *time to die.*

I trust He chose me for such a time as this (Esther 4:14). A tumultuous time of constant change, when each day brings new challenges. A speedy age when it feels hard to keep up. A season of pressure on every side. Yet each day is gift-wrapped with a deep well of abiding peace, joy, and love inside God's presence.

Newness of life is available to me each day as I spend time with God. New insight, new perspective, new hope. When I come to him willing to listen, follow, and receive instruction, I walk away with more wisdom and more peace. My doubts and fears fade as I place my trust in him, no matter how awkward I feel in this time to which I was born.

Prayer:

Heavenly Father,
Help me accept with joy this time in which you chose me to live. I want my days to be lived out in gratitude and service to you. I want to trust in you during times of obscurity and suffering. I want my life to count for your glory. Give me newness of life as I meet with you daily.
In Jesus' name, Amen.

Questions for Study and Reflection:

Choose one specific item to thank and praise God for in this time to which you have been born.

Why may God have chosen you to live during the Information Age?

When you consider Joseph's story in Genesis 30-50, what part resonates most deeply with you?

In what ways will you seize the day for God's glory today?

How will you gain newness of life by spending time alone with God this week?

Chapter 3: Planting and Harvesting

A time to plant and a time to harvest.
Ecclesiastes 3:2 NLT

Gardening is my favorite outdoor activity. I tend eight beds of vegetables and herbs, four flowerbeds, and a multitude of containers. I have learned many spiritual lessons from gardening, all centered around right timing. (If you aren't a gardener, hang in there! I promise you will gain something of value.)

In February, I get the itch to shop for seeds, and I choose the slowest-growing varieties, like pansies and strawberries, to start inside under fluorescent lights. When I started fast-growing peas inside in February, they were eight inches tall when the ground was still frozen. If I start watermelon or cucumber seeds inside, I must wait until April, because they will languish outside until the late spring sunshine warms the soil. I have to plant the right varieties at the right time, because there is *a time to plant.*

Before I begin, I must sanitize my plastic planting trays. Soil-borne diseases may cling to last year's trays and kill my seedlings before they have a chance to develop. I sanitize my tools also. A little bleach and soapy water is all it takes to prepare my planting surfaces. Likewise, if I don't include confession and repentance in my daily prayer, the diseases of sin will spread to other areas in my heart, words, and actions.

I choose new peat plugs as my growing medium. The seeds need loose, neutral soil to grow. Too heavy, and they can't set root. Too rich, and they may be burned. I soak the peat plugs in warm water. The dry discs swell and rise with moisture, and my children love watching them "grow" right before their eyes. The right soil produces healthy plants, just as the parable of the soils tells us in Luke 8.

The first green sprouts give me hope on cold, dreary winter days. Their newness of life tells me spring is coming, good wins out, and heaven is waiting. They chase away my winter blues with the promise of new life.

These tiny seedlings are so fragile. I check them several times daily to make sure they aren't too dry or too wet. Once they set four leaves, I can remove the plastic cover which serves as a greenhouse. Proper moisture is crucial but almost impossible to maintain. I always lose a few seedlings to rot or drought. That's why I plant more than I need, knowing some seeds will never reach fruition. Reaching out to others is like that. Not everyone will accept friendship or kindness, but I need to give it freely anyway, since I want to be as kind and generous as Jesus.

When the seedlings are about an inch tall, I must brush my hand over them several times a day. The gentle brushing strengthens their stems and prepares them for windy days. If I don't brush them, they will suffer upon transplanting. Like the little plants, I need "brushing" in my life too. If I don't face little trials daily, I won't be strong enough to face larger storms.

Finally, the day comes when the seedlings can be set outside. But they still must be protected. I choose a mild day and set them in a shady corner of the porch. They can't handle bright sun yet. I have to bring them in at night. I repeat this process for two weeks, setting them a bit further in the sun every day, leaving them out a little longer each day.

Planting day arrives! . I tear the bottoms off the peat pots; the roots are already protruding, ready to spread into deeper soil. I dig the hole and drop in a bit of compost as food. I set the seedling in and cover it with a cut-open milk jug. The seedlings will go into shock upon transplanting, and the milk jug dome will help them through.

Weeks pass and the seedlings astound me with rapid growth. I still must check on them daily, because pests and diseases threaten. Worms can destroy plants overnight; blight can strike a whole crop. I prepare my potions and preventive sprays. I check their soil; if it's dry to the depth of the first joint of my index finger, it's time to water. I fertilize weekly as well.

If you're not a gardener, I applaud you for hanging in here. You are probably thinking, *Gardening is WAY too much work!* I admit it's tempting to give up around August. I'm tired of the watering and spraying routines. The hot, humid weather oppresses me and the plants. But if I give up now, all my efforts from February will be in vain. I think of Galatians 6:9, *So let's not get tired of doing what is good. At just the right time we will reap a harvest of blessing if we don't give up.* I tie up the tomato vines, counting the flowers which will turn into fruits.

Harvest occurs in due time: crunchy snow peas and soft lettuce in spring. Snappy cucumbers and tender yellow squash in early summer. Fresh green beans and new potatoes in June. Succulent peppers and savory tomatoes in September. Fresh produce from my own garden compares with nothing else. All the toil is worth the first amazing taste.

I often reflect on a popular Bible teaching from Dr. Charles Stanley: We will reap what we sow, more than we sow, and later than we sow. If we plant good seeds in our faith lives, we will reap a bountiful harvest of blessing down the road. The reverse is also true. If we plant destructive seeds, they will grow into greater destruction later, not only in our own lives but in generations to come.

This has played out in my own life. When I let seeds of unforgiveness take root, they produced a greater harvest of bitterness, rage, and condemnation. It took years of hard work and therapy to destroy the roots of unforgiveness. I took on this hard work so I didn't pass the sin of unforgiveness on to my children.

With God's help, I have planted good seeds in my faith life. About fifteen years ago I began reading the Bible daily. Each day God's Word took root in my heart. This practice changed every aspect of my life for the better. It reaped a harvest of love for God, myself, and others. It reaped a harvest of knowledge and wisdom. It reaped a harvest of peace, joy, and hope. My hope is this book inspires you to seek God's word daily. You will reap a wonderful harvest!

Prayer:

Heavenly Father,
I want to reap a great harvest for you. Prepare my heart to be good soil, free of rocks and thorns, well-watered in your Word. Plant good seeds inside and help me bear the fruits of your Spirit. I want you to plant in me seeds of peace which become a harvest of righteousness (James 3:18) and seeds of righteousness which become a harvest of love (Hosea 10:12).
In Jesus' name, Amen.

Questions for Study and Reflection:

Read 1 John 1:9. How does confession help you feel clean?

Look up the parable of the soils in Luke 8. What kind of soil is in your heart?

Read James 1:2-4 with 2 Corinthians 4:17. What value do trials hold in your life?

According to 2 Corinthians 9:6, what is the best way to plant seeds?

Read Galatians 5:22-23. Which fruit of the Spirit do you desire to bear most? What do you need to plant in your heart to bear this fruit?

Chapter 4: Killing and Healing

A time to kill and a time to heal.
Ecclesiastes 3:3

I have a paralyzing fear of spiders. I don't know if I had a childhood traumatic experience, but I do know most of my nightmares feature spiders. I can't stand these scary creatures.

Since I live in the woods, I've had to readjust my lifelong fear. Spiders are everywhere in the woodlands. I appreciate the fact that they kill flies, but I still shudder when I see their webs in my windows. I'm not quite as frightened of them as when I lived in town, yet they still regularly haunt my nightmares.

One day I was working in my basement office and needed to reboot my computer. I had to check the power surge protector first, so I moved my desk around and pulled out the black surge protector, leaning close for an inspection.

I didn't realize it right away, but my face was less than a foot away from a huge tarantula, bigger than my hand. By moving the desk I disturbed it from its dark dwelling place (so near my feet!!!) and the spider stared at me with all eight eyes.

Have you ever been so terrified you screamed but no sound came out? That was me, glad I didn't scream out loud and wake my two babies up from their afternoon naps. But I was trapped in the middle of my worst nightmare ever. My husband wouldn't be home for hours. I couldn't call anyone else for help. I had to act immediately, before the spider ran out of sight and began multiplying into thousands more tarantulas IN MY OFFICE!

It was *a time to kill.* But I would have rather died than step on such a huge thing. The center of it was almost the size of an egg. No, I had to get creative, and fast.

I found an open glue trap in the closet. I grabbed a broom and stuck the bristles on one edge of the sticky surface. Then, from the four-foot broom handle distance, I slid the glue trap toward the spider and got its legs on there. I murmur-screamed as I dragged the enormous spider toward the patio door, forcing myself to watch and make sure it didn't escape. I left the whole thing out in the woods, broom and all, and came inside trembling with fear and a measure of relief.

Hours later, I worked up the courage to retrieve my broom. The spider was gone! I hoped and prayed it had become a snack for a wandering raccoon, and hadn't simply pried its legs off the glue trap and slinked back into the woods to reproduce. I have yet to see another spider so gigantic on our property, and here's hoping that stays true as I inspect the underside of my desk again. Yikes!

Seriously now: a time to kill. How often is that necessary in our day-to-day, sanitized, safety-driven lives? A time to kill flies, spiders, or mosquitoes, maybe, but *a time to kill* seems more fitting for an action movie than in everyday life for a Christian.

When I've killed creatures, it's due to accident or necessity. Many times I've accidently killed a squirrel running across the street because it was more dangerous to swerve than keep moving. I kill mosquitoes so they don't bite me, and other vermin so they don't carry diseases into our home. And yes, I kill spiders so their population doesn't overrun its proper placement in the local ecosystem.

What I truly need to kill is hidden on the inside. In the past, I tried the wrong methods to kill my evil desires. Ignoring them didn't work. Making excuses and covering them up only intensified their power. Blaming my temptations on a difficult childhood also didn't weaken their hold.

This is what worked: I exposed my evil desires to the light of God's word. I admitted their hold over me and took responsibility for my indulgence. I sought out healing in Jesus. When the evil desires flared up again, I began fighting back with the truth of scripture.

Over time, God helped me put those evil desires to death. I faced a long, difficult process, but now those desires no longer affect my daily living. They had to be rooted out from the base and completely destroyed for me to be whole again. Healed.

Healing requires time and vulnerability. Healing doesn't happen overnight. There is *a time to heal,* and God will call you to it. I had to peel back the layers of why, when, and how to get to the basis of my evil desires. God had to cut them out of my life, and it hurt. Getting to the truth of why the desires were there in the first place exposed my long-held loneliness, insecurity, and feelings of unworthiness. Those were raw wounds I had kept carefully hidden for decades. Exposing them, even to God, felt risky.

But I knew deep down I would never get better until I exposed my wounds to God's healing touch. I knew only He held the power to heal them completely. I trusted Him to hold me in His arms during that painful process. The salves He applied sometimes burned. I had to change patterns which had brought me false comfort for years. I had to reprogram the way I spoke to myself. I had to retrain the way I thought about others who had hurt me. I had to name the pain, forgive, grieve, and let go.

Healing came slowly but surely. I needed the help of a counselor to receive full healing, and I highly recommend counseling to anyone having problems which are interfering with having a normal, healthy life. I spent about four years in counseling to move from a place of fear and passivity to a place of emotional security.

I have emotional scars now which will always be a part of me. But they are no longer open wounds. They tell a story of survival and triumph through God's healing power. I give him all the glory.

Prayer:

Heavenly Father,
You are my healer. Send me your Spirit to show me which evil desires need to be put to death in my heart. Grant me healing in your perfect timing and in your perfect ways. I need your help and your guidance to become a whole, healthy person.
In Jesus' name, Amen.

Questions for Study and Reflection:

Which fear paralyzes you, and why?

Read Colossians 3. Which one of the sins listed here is a struggle for you? How can God help you kill your evil desires?

Referring to Colossians 3 again, what gives you the power to overcome sinful desires? What action can you take to pursue one of the godly attributes listed in verses 12-17?

When did you need a time of healing? How did God help you in that time?

Read Luke 6:19. Why do you think healing was such an important part of Jesus' earthly ministry, when the results were only temporary?

Chapter 5: Tearing Down and Building Up

A time to tear down and a time to build up.
Ecclesiastes 3:3 NLT

I stayed home the day they tore down the smokehouse on the family farm. I couldn't bear to watch.

The smokehouse was the last vestige of old times, when my great-grandparents inhabited the property. As the oldest great-grandchild, I still hold dear memories of butchering days.

When I smell hickory smoke, I am transported back to a winter day, age three. The farm is a hubbub of activity. My daddy's family is all gathered to help. The ladies are gathered around the kitchen table, dusting fresh hams with salt and sugar. The men carry the hams to the smokehouse and hang them up in the dark wooden rooms. Smoke stings my eyes but I like the smell. I've tasted this ham before. It's very good with scalloped potatoes and glazed carrots.

Butchering days were memorable to me because it's when the family gathered together, working for a common goal. United. Stable. These memories spoke deeply to me as a child of divorce. I'm thankful for memories of family unity before my family splintered apart at age four. Those memories planted seeds of hope in my heart for my own family someday.

Something inside me from way back resists tearing down. Tearing down feels wrong, wasteful, destructive, harmful. Tearing down reminds me of too much past pain.

The time had arrived to tear down the smokehouse. It hadn't been used as a smokehouse for years. The price for pork had dropped so low, my great-grandparents stopped raising pigs. After they died and my grandparents moved onto the property, the smokehouse was a rickety home for feral cats. It was an eyesore, no longer useful.

After family members tore the smokehouse down, we had a new view of the pond. An unobstructed view. A peaceful view. A view which reached further and wider. The tearing down made way for something better.

I love watching remodeling shows like *Fixer Upper* because they show me the good side of tearing down. Demo Day arrives, when they tear down walls and tear out cabinets to make way for open floor plans and flowing spaces. They build up to recreate something new, beautiful, and useful.

My favorite episodes are when they preserve a brick wall, a beam, or a stained glass window from the old structure and incorporate it into the new design. They don't completely tear down the old, but they preserve a remnant to give the new owners a sense of the house's history.

My husband is a builder by trade. He says it's much easier and less expensive to tear down and rebuild rather than restore. He agrees tearing down can be wasteful. But if you take time to repurpose the items, tearing down can bring newness of life.

Once he was remodeling a home. The owners had a huge, solid oak cabinet set they told him to give away or throw away. He came home and measured the opening between the windows in our family room. The cabinet set fit perfectly, with only a half-inch of space on either side. We had a $2,500 price quote from a cabinetmaker for a similar design, and were getting by with a cheap television cabinet and two decorator tables until we could afford better. The cabinet set was an enormous blessing to us, even when it was part of someone else's tearing down.

Building up is exciting, fresh, fun. Tearing down is hard, messy, and painful. But often, building up isn't possible without first tearing down.

Tearing down old dreams to make room for new possibilities. When I was young I dreamed of being an artist, writer, musician, and actress. My teachers told me it wasn't possible to pursue all those dreams with equal intensity. They said I would naturally gravitate toward my strongest love over time. Their words have proven true. Writing has been my consistent pursuit over the last 20 years. Giving up those other dreams made one dream more tangible.

Tearing down high expectations to accept a healthier reality. I tend to expect much from myself and my loved ones. This often puts a strain on my self-esteem and my relationships. I have learned tearing myself or others down is never a good application of this chapter's theme verse. Building myself and others up is in alignment with God's will. When I feel those expectations rising high, I grant myself grace, saying, "Everyone makes mistakes. You'll get through this." And when others let me down, I ask myself if perhaps I was expecting too much and if I should silently let them off the hook. Building up is my path toward accepting a healthier reality.

Tearing down childish feelings to make room for adult thinking. I hate to admit it, but I often secretly view myself as a victim. I'm sure some of this came out of childhood scenarios when I faced trials without any power to change them. But I am mature enough to take my thoughts captive to Christ and view myself as more than a conqueror by his love. In 1 Corinthians 13, the apostle Paul wrote he put childish ways behind him as he became a man, just as we will someday tear down our limited understanding of God and know him fully in heaven.

Building up is an adventure. In 2002 my husband and I purchased the wooded property which would become our homestead. We cleared the trees and built the house with the help of family and friends on nights and weekends. Each new stage held excitement and promise. Setting trusses gave the house shape. Hanging drywall made the spaces feel like real rooms. Fitting the planks of the wood floor together was the biggest, most important puzzle I'd ever attempted, especially between feedings of our newborn baby boy.

We held a huge party to thank everyone who helped in September 2004, sixteen months after the building process got underway. Many people gave their time, sweat, and weekends up for us, and we were deeply grateful. Everyone enjoyed seeing how their efforts had paid off in our beautiful new home in the woods. Building up gives a sense of accomplishment.

Building up leads to more building up. In the past twelve years, we have finished the basement, transformed a gully into a large pond, added an addition, remodeled several rooms, and cleaned up the woods. When we built the house, we were just catching the vision of what our property would be in the future.

Ephesians 4:11-16 speaks of the way the church works as a body to build itself up. All parts of the body are joined by Christ, just as all parts of a house are held together with nails and mortar. All parts work together in love to grow to maturity. Mature believers work hard to build one another up and avoid tearing each other down. The time for tearing down in the church is reserved for building projects, not people. Let's work together to make the church a stronger, built-up place.

Prayer:

Heavenly Father,
I want to be known as a builder in your kingdom. Tear down my foolishness to make way for maturity. Tear down my sinful habits to make room for holy ones. Tear down my pride to make a place for humility. Build up in me a desire for following your will. Teach me how to build others up in your church. Show me who needs building up today.
In Jesus' name, Amen.

Questions for Study and Reflection:

Read Revelation 21:5. How is Jesus tearing down the old and making something new in you today?

Read Isaiah 28:1-6, focusing on verse 5. How does God's promise to preserve a remnant, even in a time of tearing down, give you comfort?

How might your process of tearing down benefit someone else?

How does God want you to use your words, according to Ephesians 4:29?

When you read 1 Corinthians 13:11-12, what ways do you need to tear down? What needs building up in your heart?

Chapter 6: Crying and Laughing

A time to cry and a time to laugh.
Ecclesiastes 3:4 NLT

When God knit me together, he wove in plenty of purple melancholy threads.

When God knit my middle son together, he wove in plenty of sunshine yellow sanguine threads.

I know sadness well. My boy knows happiness well. God knew what he was doing when he placed us together in this family. We balance each other out. As an artist, I know purple and yellow are complementary colors. Put yellow daffodils next to purple pansies in spring, and both colors pop. Place sunflowers in a vase with deep purple statice, and you have the loveliest late summer arrangement. These opposites not only balance each other, they enhance one another.

Crying and laughing sometimes go together. I'm sure you've laughed so hard you've cried. There is a time for both, and sometimes they coincide.

I've got *a time to cry* down pat. I've shed many tears, mostly in private. I'm not one to cry at the drop of a hat, but one who feels everything deeply.

Sometimes I need to cry to feel better, to vent feelings and move on. My children were like this as toddlers. When they were tired and cranky, they needed to cry before napping to release the tension before they relaxed at naptime. I still feel that way when I'm stressed.

Sometimes my tears spring up from a deep reservoir. When I was sorting through my painful teenage years in therapy, I recalled how I would sit in the basement bathroom every night and listen to the same cassette tapes over and over. A song which gave me glimmers of hope in the depths of my depression was "Everybody Hurts" by R.E.M. That song helped me hold on when I was tempted to despair.

During my healing process, I downloaded the song from ITunes. While the song played on my phone, tears poured over my face. I wasn't sobbing; the tears simply flooded out from a deep place inside which had never received healing. Those tears helped release pain so deep wounds could be healed.

Sometimes my tears are sparked by joy. Just this week I had a wonderful, reconciling phone conversation. Afterward I was vacuuming up dead leaves from my houseplants and suddenly became overcome with sobs as the melody of a lovely song sprang into my thoughts. A song of rejoicing sung by my church choir, based on Psalm 30:11. Sorrow into dancing...we will discuss that change in the next chapter. My sobs were from another deep place—a place which had not given up hope despite a hard situation. A place of rejoicing. A transformed place, thanks to God's miraculous work.

A verse from which I take great comfort is this one:

You keep track of all my sorrows. You have collected all my tears in your bottle. You have recorded each one in your book.
Psalm 56:8 NLT

My tears matter to God. He doesn't tell me to stop crying when I need to let them out. He doesn't shun my tears. He collects them and sets him on his kitchen windowsill, like I set little cobalt blue bottles on mine. In a strange and wonderful way, my tears are God's treasures. How a holy God values my pain, I don't really understand. But knowing so helps me trust in him, because he is tender with my hurts. He ordains *a time to cry*, and I am grateful.

Last year I read a fascinating Facebook post[1] by one of my favorite authors, Dr. Henry Cloud. He posted pictures by Rose-Lynn Fisher[2] of the different molecular structure of four kinds of tears: grief, laughter, onions, and change. Here's my description of the photos:

Onion tears (provoked by irritants) look like spreading nets or ferns, almost protective.
Grief tears look like messed-up subdivisions with broken streets and waylaid development, spread far apart.
Laughter tears are loose and fluid, bursting out of formation.

Tears of change show disruption within the overall pattern and an adaptation to a new pattern.
All tears are comprised of salt and water plus other substances. Emotional tears contain a natural painkiller.[3] Isn't God's grace amazing? He provides real healing for us in our tears. That's why he ordains *a time to cry.*

God gives us physical benefits in laughter as well. Laughter releases feel-good endorphins, gives your heart and lungs a workout, stimulates oxygen circulation and muscle relaxation. Laughing may also strengthen your immune system, provide pain relief, improve your coping skills, and boost your mood.[4]

I laugh most often with my children. When they laugh in their melodic voices, I can't help but laugh myself. To get them laughing, I chase them and tickle them. They love it! We also laugh together by playing board games. I want them to remember our times of laughing together when they have their own families.

As I was writing, my sanguine boy came up behind me with a new Christmas game, titled Gas Out. You can imagine the sounds which came out of this silly blob shape he placed in my chair. His peals of laughter rang through the house and I knew it was *a time to laugh* together.

I am serious to a fault. That's why I choose to spend time with funny friends and watch comedies regularly. My violet tears need to be balanced out with golden laughter. It's especially good when they overlap. My insides are healed and God laughs along.

I read this wonderful verse in Revelation this morning:

He will wipe every tear from their eyes, and there will be no more death or sorrow or crying or pain. All these things are gone forever. Revelation 21:4

Isn't it comforting to realize one day there will be no more time to cry, and an endless time to laugh? I'm praising God today for this heavenly glimpse!

Prayer:

Heavenly Father,
Thank you for collecting my tears in a bottle. Thank you for caring about my hurts. Thank you also for the gift of laughter. You are so wise to create times for both, and even to ordain times of overlap. Help me know when someone needs me to cry along. Help me know when it's time to inspire a laugh to lift someone up. Move me forward with faith that one day no crying will be necessary.
In Jesus' name, Amen.

Questions for Study and Reflection:

Write out Ecclesiastes 7:3. Meditate on this verse and ask yourself if you agree, and why.

Read James 4:8-10. For what purpose does God sometimes want us to change our laughter into mourning?

Read Ecclesiastes 10:19. What feasts in your life have inspired laughter?

When you read John 11:34-36, what does it mean to you that Jesus took time to cry?

Read Psalm 126:5. How does God transform your tears into joy?

Chapter 7: Grieving and Dancing

A time to grieve and a time to dance.
Ecclesiastes 3:4 NLT

In the fall of 2012, my beloved grandpa passed away after a long fallout from a stroke. That began the first grieving period of my adult life.

A Stephen Minister from my church began sending booklets on grief every month or so. I began to get a grasp on this strange, overwhelming, fluid emotion. An emotion which suddenly sprang up at odd moments, when I thought I was perfectly under control. It welled up at a parade, because I attended so many with him. It bubbled up at the scent of pancakes, because he cooked so many for us. It gushed out at the sight of a mall Santa Claus, since Grandpa had served as a Santa for so many years.

Grief briefly overtook me when I saw my great-uncle at my workplace one day, and his voice and mannerisms seemed like an exact replica of Grandpa. I ran to a back room to wipe away tears, then the grief ebbed as quickly as it had arrived.

I heard a sermon by Dr. Adrian Rogers during that period. He said grief is a love word. You can't grieve someone or something you never loved.

When I read those books on grief from my church, random memories surfaced from a high school relationship which never resolved. I felt ridiculous and ashamed, mulling over memories 20 years later as a wife and mother of three. The memories began interfering with my daily life. But now I can see how God was using those grief books to draw repressed memories to the surface and slowly heal them once and for all.

I had struggled with a thought-life problem over this relationship for a long time. I couldn't forgive myself, I couldn't stop asking why, and I couldn't stop wondering about different outcomes. If I had only been healthier. If I had only been happier. If only… My thoughts swirled around this relationship no matter how hard I tried to suppress it. I felt frustrated, confused, and stuck. The problem didn't diminish, no matter how much I talked about it, wrote about it, prayed about it, ignored it, or cursed it.

By grief book #4 I gave up the struggle. I prayed, "God, I guess you want me to focus on grieving this past relationship which never really materialized. I feel foolish, but here goes." Finally, by walking through the steps of grief, I reached resolution. The stronghold was broken and I could move forward.
Grief has several well-known stages of change. I walked through them in 2012, when I also realized I had been walking back-and-forth between them as a child of divorce for decades. Here's how my journey looked in these situations:

Denial. I don't have a problem. I've got this under control. Yeah, so bad things happen. No one has to know. I don't have to share it. It's fine, just between me and God.
The results of denial: stress-related psoriasis and eczema, bingeing, negative self-talk, obsessive thoughts

Anger. I'm not an angry person. I'm known for being calm. Anyway if I'm angry it's not that big of a deal. It doesn't change anything, so what's the point?
The results of repressed anger: self-destructive behaviors, snapping at loved ones, discontent, depression

Bargaining. If I'm good, if I'm perfect, if I'm under complete control, bad things won't get to me as much. I'll be able to handle this. I've got to work harder at being balanced, at having it all together, at not being needy. Then I'll feel better.
The results of bargaining: setup for failure, self-condemnation, feelings of hopelessness, increased need

Sadness. This pain is overtaking my life. It's hard to admit, but I'm desperate for help. I must feel this sad because I really cared about this person. If I didn't care this much, it wouldn't be so hard. I've got to reach out.
The results of sadness: honesty, community, healing, hope

Acceptance. I learned from this. I didn't simply survive—I'm thriving now. I'm healthier. I'm stronger. The pain doesn't have a death grip on me anymore. It's a battle scar now, and I can reveal it to help others.

This is why God gives us *a time to grieve.* Healing and wholeness are on the side of acceptance. It took me years to arrive at the acceptance phase, particularly when I was grieving several live relationships which may never be truly satisfying. But acceptance is a beautiful way to live, and if grief was the price I had to pay, it was worth the cost.

You turned my wailing into dancing;
you removed my sackcloth and clothed me with joy,
that my heart may sing your praises and not be silent.
LORD my God, I will praise you forever.
Psalm 30:11-12

When grief retreats, it's *a time to dance.* If I'm dancing, I'm at a celebration. A banquet, a party, a wedding. A joyful gathering.

My dancing memories: tap-dancing as a three-year-old, glittery and fancy. Learning to polka in Grandma's living room. Spinning around a wooden floor on New Year's Eve at an old-fashioned German dance hall. Swaying with my brand-new husband to our song, "Can't Take My Eyes Off You." Teaching our children the two-step to Chris LeDoux in our kitchen.

Happy memories. Joyful memories. God sweeps away the sadness to help us trust him. To call us to him in praise.

I want to share my friend Mary Ann's story of grief and joy. In two years, catastrophe rocked her world. Her mother succumbed to dementia. Her brother nearly died from the same disease which took her father and another brother. And Mary Ann herself was diagnosed with cancer. Despair threatened to steal her joy.

But Mary Ann began to write within her despair. Pursuing her long-held dream of writing gave her newness of life. Her sibling relationships were redefined and strengthened. She renewed her faith by studying scriptures of comfort.

Mary Ann says, "Little by little, I am discovering the season of laughter and dancing which follows weeping and despair. Perhaps I am transitioning into a deeper likeness of Jesus." I believe our times of grieving and dancing do just that.

Prayer:

Heavenly Father,
You are so wise to grant me a time to grieve when my hearts is broken. I pray for those who I know are grieving today. Wrap them in the comfort of your arms. Help them to sense your loving presence. Help them walk through the stages of grief so they might soon reach the season of dancing, in praise to you. In Jesus' name, Amen.

Questions for Study and Reflection:

What has been your most difficult season of grief?

Which stage of grief is hardest for you, and why?

Read John 16:19-21. Why did the world rejoice when the disciples were grieving? How did Jesus turn their grief into joy?

Look up Jeremiah 31:12-13. How has God transformed your sorrows into dancing?

Think of a person who is grieving today. What one step can you take to help them?

Chapter 8: Scattering and Gathering

A time to scatter stones and a time to gather stones.
Ecclesiastes 3:5 NLT

The Old Testament is full of stories about stones, both scattering and gathering. How do we understand this in today's context? The way I see it, most of the scattering then was about smashing altars to false gods. Most of the gathering was about building and remembering. That's how we'll look at it in this chapter.

When I plugged in the word "smash" in the search box on biblegateway.com, dozens of references popped up. God told his people to smash the sacred stones, destroy altars, and cut down poles meant for worshipping foreign gods. The writers used vivid verbs: smash, cut, break, destroy, demolish. I envision bits of rubble scattered about once the destruction was over. Perhaps the Israelites gathered those bits and sprinkled them around the pagan temples to prove not even a pile would be left. The stones were smashed into dust.

Recently I watched *Indiana Jones and the Temple of Doom* for the first time in years. Indy was on a quest to steal sacred stones from a pagan temple. He watched the pagans complete a ritual of human sacrifice, then he crept up to the altar to swipe the stones. When he took hold of the glowing stones, they exerted bizarre power over him, coercing him comply with pagan plans to offer his girlfriend as a sacrifice. Right before she was lowered into the fiery lava pit, Indy was awakened from the stones' spell and saved the day.

I think that's the image most of us have of idol worship. Mysterious artifacts, strange rituals, and weird sacrifices. Something ancient pagans did. Not us. Not civilized, 21st century believers.

When I was in Bible Study Fellowship, we often had discussions about current day idols. They are slick and sneaky, more sophisticated than the stone, metal, or wooden idols in Old Testament times. Your idol may be something positive like items on this list:

- The person you're dating
- Your spouse

- Family members
- Friendships
- Your smartphone
- Television
- Social media
- Your job
- Your health
- Your looks
- Your finances
- Your hobbies
- Your church
- Your ministry
- Your stuff
- Food or drink

Anything which takes first place in your life, other than God, may be an idol. Anything you cling to in times of desperation may become your idol.

Remember in Chapter 3 when I wrote even a good plant can be a weed if it's growing where something else has a rightful place? Idols are like that too. Family is a wonderful blessing, but if it supersedes God's place, it may be an idol. Same goes for church. At one time, I put more energy into my church activities than I did at home. That's okay for a brief season tied to a project, but not long-term. I had to adjust my thinking on these good things which came close to becoming idols.

What I found underneath my sometimes-idol of reading, for example, is the desire to escape. Underneath the desire to escape is a desire for peace. Peace is a healthy pursuit, but not when it comes at the expense of spending time with my family or taking care of my household. And sometimes, reading gets in the way of my time with God. If I don't keep reading on a short leash, it easily creeps into my heart as an idol.

So do I really need to smash and scatter the stones of idols in my heart? Can't I live alongside them and not have to make a mess of smashing them to bits?

When I begin feeling convicted about an item on the list above, I begin rationalizing. Take television. I used to watch a soapy drama one night a week. The content got racy and I felt torn between guilt and a desire to keep watching. Week after week went by and my discomfort grew. I knew it wasn't good for me but I kept saying to myself, "There's a lot worse on TV I don't ever watch. One show a week won't hurt. I'm an adult, after all. I can handle this."

When the storyline took more graphic turns, I finally deleted my DVR timer. I feel much better now I don't have that TV show on my conscience. In a way, I smashed that idol by refusing to watch anymore. But I also felt ashamed because I didn't listen to the Holy Spirit's promptings to stop watching sooner. I need to be honest about idols creeping in at the beginning, not at the end. I do need to smash them to bits right away.

Ask God to show you what idols have sneaked into your heart and mind. Ask him if you are holding anything too closely, especially good things. Ask him if it is *a time to scatter stones.* I like these verses and often incorporate them in my time of confession:

Search me, God, and know my heart;
test me and know my anxious thoughts.
See if there is any offensive way in me,
and lead me in the way everlasting.
Psalm 139:23-24

When God reveals an idol to you, think about how you might smash and scatter those stones you've made sacred. If it's a relationship, try branching out and find additional outlets for giving and receiving love. If it's technology, try setting a timer on how much you use it.

Ask yourself what desire lies underneath the idol. Maybe it is one of these intangibles:

- Comfort
- Security
- Beauty
- Love
- Respect
- Acceptance
- Fulfillment
- Power
- Control

How can the desire for these intangibles be transformed within your relationship to God? How can they be set in their proper placement in your heart, with God at the center?

A time to gather stones can be about building, which we will talk about in Chapter 15, or about remembrance. In Joshua 4 the Israelites are crossing the Jordan River. God instructs them to gather twelve stones from the Jordan River as stones of remembrance, one stone for each of the tribes of Israel. God dried up the river while the ark of the covenant passed through. Then Joshua addressed the people:

"In the future when your descendants ask their parents, 'What do these stones mean?' tell them, 'Israel crossed the Jordan on dry ground.' For the LORD your God dried up the Jordan before you until you had crossed over. The LORD your God did to the Jordan what he had done to the Red Sea when he dried it up before us until we had crossed over. He did this so that all the peoples of the earth might know that the hand of the LORD is powerful and so that you might always fear the LORD your God." Joshua 4:21-24

God wanted them to see the stones and remember His power, faithfulness, and commitment to His own people. He wanted future generations of Israelites to see how He had provided for their ancestors and preserved their heritage. He wanted to inspire their trust in all their seasons of change.

I am teaching my children to remember times of God's faithfulness by setting up mental memorial stones. We talk about times when God has provided for us financially. We remember times he protected us in storms, both severe thunderstorms with tornado warnings and even scarier emotional storms. We reminisce on ways loved ones have shown us examples of faith. I want to set up mental markers for them while they are young so they will learn to trust God when their life seasons change.

When spring comes again, we will set up stones in our garden and mark memories on them with permanent markers. My daughter has a fairy garden on our porch. We can lay a tiny stone path of blessings, little memorials of God's faithfulness. Then she can see how God has walked alongside us, whether we were scattering stones or gathering them.

Prayer:

Heavenly Father,
I can't always tell the difference between a healthy desire and an idolatrous desire. Search my heart and find any offensive way in me, Lord, and help me overcome my unbelief in your all-sufficiency. With your power I can smash my idols and scatter their dust. Help me identify the times of your faithfulness, so I can gather stones of remembrance and grow in faith and trust.
In Jesus' name, Amen.

Questions for Study and Reflection:

When you consider the list of possible idols, which one stands out to you?

Which intangible idea lies underneath that idol?

What practical steps might you take to scatter the sacred stones of your heart idols?

Skim Exodus 28:1-30. What do these precious memory stones signify? What is the significance of where the stones were to be placed?

Read 1 Peter 2:4-6. How is God gathering you like a stone, and for what purpose?

Chapter 9: Embracing and Turning Away

A time to embrace, and a time to turn away.
Ecclesiastes 3:5 NLT

This week I had time to run a few errands while my oldest son had basketball practice. Pay my tax bill—check. Run to the recycling center—check. Exchange a scarf—last item to check off.

As soon as I entered the quaint uptown shop, a voice called out to me. Eyes I hadn't seen in over 20 years smiled at me, and my old friend wrapped me a warm, lingering hug.

I live in the same small town where I grew up. It's not uncommon to see people I know almost every time I'm out and about. But an embrace? That's uncommon, and delightfully welcome (at least from this particular friend).

This friend and I were inseparable in kindergarten. She was the happy-go-lucky free spirit and I was the scholarly good girl. We made an interesting pair because we both liked to read and learn. We rode the bus home together and talked all the way home. When a boy behind us wouldn't stop pulling on my braided pigtails, she giggled and said, "I think he likes you." I thought she must know since she had brothers and I didn't. I asked for my hair to be cut in a bob like hers, thereby avoiding any more teasing.

We grew apart when we went to different elementary schools. But our friendship revived in high school when we worked together on the school newspaper and speech team. I hadn't seen her since she moved away for college.

In the little shop this week, we talked about our writing projects and promised to support each other. I think it's wonderful that we are still very different. She's still a free spirit and I'm still a good girl. But we still have enough in common to be friends and we have an old, cherished bond.
When I consider a time to embrace and a time to turn away, I can't help but review how much my friendships have evolved and changed over the years. I am richly blessed with several friendships which have lasted for over three decades. Many other friendships have lasted a short season while others faded completely.

When I was newly pregnant with my first baby, I worked as a temp at two different offices. In one office God placed me among two very pregnant women, and I enjoyed learning how future months in my pregnancy might take shape. Their stories normalized my fears. At the other office, an experienced mother shared stories of raising her five-year-old son. I was hungry for knowledge about parenting, and this dear woman offered me many good ideas and inspired my hope. I saw those ladies maybe once or twice after my temp assignments were complete, but I am thankful for the brief season of their encouraging friendships. God's timing was perfect.

Other friendships faded completely due to changed interests, different schedules, or opposing viewpoints. I let one friendship drop off when I got tired of the toxic patterns. Sometimes friends have stopped connecting with me for reasons I don't understand and will probably never know. The time to embrace and time to turn away can be a tricky, painful dance in friendships.

As a college English major, I remember being fascinated by Dante's *Inferno*. His masterpiece describes different levels of torture in the afterlife. The canto I found most interesting depicts two lovers in an eternal embrace. At that time, I desired nothing more than a romantic relationship, and the idea of a torturous eternal embrace seemed incomprehensible.

Since I'm older and a bit wiser, I think I now understand the deeper meaning beneath Dante's metaphor. None of us is capable of enduring full relationship intensity all the time. We need time to live normal lives not dominated by passion. Passion and intimacy has its place—there is *a time to embrace.* That time is glorious and heavenly. But also, we need breathing room—there is *a time to turn away.*

A time to turn away from my quest to connect. *A time to turn away* from people and projects, and *a time to embrace* God alone. Turning away from my intense pursuit of validation in friends' words, and turning toward validation in God's word alone.

Psalm 139 tells me I am known through and through, carefully created, fearfully and wonderfully made.

In Ephesians 2 I learn I am alive in Christ, saved by grace, created to do good works, reconciled to God, and a dwelling place for the Holy Spirit.

In Romans 8 I find I am no longer condemned, but led by the Spirit. I am God's heir, and He is working all things together for my good. I am more than a conqueror through God's great love.

Based on 1 Peter 2:9, I am chosen, royal, set apart, and a special possession to God.

Time in God's word gives me newness of life like nothing else can. When I reserve time for God I feel strengthened, affirmed, settled, and connected to rivers of truth underneath the surface of daily life.

Blessed is the one
who does not walk in step with the wicked
or stand in the way that sinners take
or sit in the company of mockers,
but whose delight is in the law of the LORD,
and who meditates on his law day and night.
That person is like a tree planted by streams of water,
which yields its fruit in season
and whose leaf does not wither—
whatever they do prospers. Psalm 1:1-3

Do you regularly take time to embrace God's word? Do you see yourself as a tree planted by the water of His truth, so you may have newness of life in whatever life season you face? You will yield fruit and not wither, so long as you are walking closely with God.

The Bible warns against turning away from God. There is never a right time to turn away from him. Consider this scripture:

For I command you this day to love the LORD your God and to keep his commands, decrees, and regulations by walking in his ways. If you do this, you will live and multiply, and the LORD your God will bless you and the land you are about to enter and occupy.

But if your heart turns away and you refuse to listen, and if you are drawn away to serve and worship other gods, then I warn you now that you will certainly be destroyed. You will not live a long, good life in the land you are crossing the Jordan to occupy. Deuteronomy 30:16-18 NLT

As we discussed in the previous chapter, when we allow anything, even good things like friendship, to draw us away from God and become an idol, we miss out on newness of life. I encourage you to plant yourself by the waters of God's word so you can flourish in every season.

Prayer:

Heavenly Father,
Thank you to ministering to me through my friendships. May they always be sources of blessing and encouragement, but never draw me away from you. Lord, I want to be a tree planted by the water of your word, drawing sustenance from you daily. Help me make time to turn away from everything else and focus on what you are teaching me.
In Jesus' name, Amen.

Questions for Study and Reflection:

Which of your friendships brings you great blessing?

Is there a friendship from which you need to turn away? Why?

What time of day is best for you to turn away from all else besides time with God?

Read 1 Samuel 12:20-21. Why should you turn away from idols? How does God want you to focus your energy instead?

Read John 4:7-14 with John 7:38. How is God's word like living water, and in what ways might God want you to share it?

Chapter 10: Searching and Stopping

A time to search and a time to quit searching.
Ecclesiastes 3:6 NLT

One of the first gifts my husband gave me when we were dating was a pair of gold hoop earrings. They were just the right size, not too small or too big, and beveled to catch the light. I wore them often, and created a tradition of wearing them at the birth of each of our three children.

One evening this past summer, I got home from my son's ballgame and looked in the mirror as I got ready for bed. One of my dear hoop earrings was missing. I am not the kind to absentmindedly misplace items. In fact, I am borderline OCD about checking everything three times. I knew it had fallen out somewhere. I began retracing my steps, enlisting the help of my family to search for the missing earring. I showed them the match and we all had eyes peeled for a little gold hoop.

I had noticed the last few times while wearing it that the prongs which held the post in place seemed loose. Perhaps if I had tightened the prongs, I would have saved my earring from getting lost. I pushed the discouraging thought aside as I surveyed the stairs.

We got down on hands and knees all over the house. We combed through the carpet on the vehicle interior. We checked it all again. I called off the search because it was past bedtime, but my desperation rose.

In the morning, I asked my oldest son to return to the ballpark for one final search. People with metal detectors come through that area fairly regularly, looking for coins or jewelry to pawn. My hopes were low, but I wanted to try once more to find the little gold earring which had been mine for sixteen years.

We looked all over the grass, sidewalks, and gravel parking area three times. Finally, I decided we had spent enough time looking, and my hope of finding the earring was laid to rest. I still haven't found it, and I doubt I ever will.

I have always been sentimental, keeping things which aren't necessarily meaningful or valuable to anyone else but me. I think I gained this trait in childhood, when things filled in the space of love I felt was missing. If I held an old card which said, "I Love You," it was proof of love even when I didn't feel loved. Letters, wrappers, doodads, bookmarks, stickers, and ticket stubs became a trail of love evidence.

When I lost my earring, though, I didn't feel devastated as I would have in childhood. My sense of self-worth was no longer tied up in material proof. More on this in a bit, but first, consider these questions:

When have you gone on a search for something out of your reach?

What happened to make you give up searching?

Here's what told me it was time to stop searching for love, and keeping a desperate scrapbook of proof: the healing process I mentioned in Chapter 4. After giving up this earring search, the more I reflected upon it, the prouder I was of myself. This incident occurred in summer 2016, nearly sixteen years into our marriage. Fifteen of those years were very rocky. So many times, friends and family and even counselors would gravely say, "The problems you share are beyond ordinary, day-to-day marriage issues." That was strangely comforting in a way, because I thought, *If every other married couple experiences this much heartache, marriage is a huge letdown.* But if we were the oddball, secretly super-monstrous couple, I thought, *This level of heartache is probably appropriate.*

For fifteen years I desperately clung to every scrap of human love I could find, much like I did as a child. But in the months leading up to April 2015, I reached the end of my healing process and let go. I stopped searching for redemptive love in my imperfect husband and threw myself at the feet of the cross. I gave up my quest, as God instructed me to do. His word became my life-giving fountain, just as Jesus promised to the woman at the well in John 4, a woman also desperately searching for love.

When my husband and I separated for a brief period in April 2015, in one sense I lived out my ultimate nightmare as a child of divorce. But a mysterious, powerful peace stole over me and carried me through, a greater peace than I had ever experienced before. God reassured me in those weeks He would love me, support me, provide for me, and sustain me no matter what happened, when my future truly seemed dire and hopeless. My proof of being loved and worthy was in God's love for me, no longer in what imperfect humans were willing to offer.

On the front side of your stopped search is grief and pain. On the back side of your stopped search is perfect peace which passes all understanding.

But you must be willing to let go and trust God as you stop searching. Trust in His character, timing, and sovereignty over your life. Trust Him not to let you down when everyone and everything already has.

If you are in a season of searching, ask God if it's a wise search (asking, seeking, knocking in Matthew 7) or a fruitless one. Ask him if you should keep searching or stop.

If you are in a season of stopping a search, trust God with your whole heart. I trusted Him with everything in my time of greatest crisis, and He made my trembling faith as sure and strong as a mountain. All because I gave up searching for something out of my reach—something imperfect God never wanted me to find anyway.

Prayer:

Heavenly Father,
Is what I'm searching for wise or fruitless? If I'm asking, seeking, and knocking in places where I should stop, please let me know. Help me to trust you with my whole heart and seek redemption and salvation only in you.
In Jesus' name, Amen.

Questions for Study and Reflection:

Where does God search? See 1 Chronicles 28:9.

What kind of search does God want us to undertake, according to Psalm 4:4?

Which person of the Trinity has special searching ability? See 1 Corinthians 2:10.

Who does God search for, according to Ezekiel 34:16?

Referring to the previous question, how do the parables in Luke 15 prove your answer? Which parable is your favorite, and why?

Chapter 11: Keeping and Throwing Away

A time to keep and a time to throw away.
Ecclesiastes 3:6

When I first planted my vegetable garden, I started with a row of sixteen strawberry plants. I didn't know then strawberry plants put out several runners each year, and one plant can quickly turn into six or ten.

Within three years my original strawberry plants had turned into 100 square feet of strawberry crops. I let them grow rampant because my children had so much fun picking berries. Every other day for three weeks, we picked four quarts of berries. I froze many bags of berries and turned more into jam. We were in strawberry heaven.

By year five the strawberries had overrun into spaces I needed for tomatoes, peppers, and lettuce. I had already given away as many plants as people wanted. Digging up the rest and transplanting them to a new bed was too much work. I felt discouraged by the enormity of the task. I feared wasting perfectly good plants, but I didn't know what else to do.

I set the lawn mower on the lowest height and took it to my garden. I felt like I was committing a crime against my garden by mowing down healthy plants. A quote from a gardening magazine came to mind as I worked my way through half the garden: "Any plant in the wrong place is a weed." My strawberries had become like dandelions, unwanted and unwelcome where other plants need room to grow.

A new, unexpected feeling came over me as I finished mowing: pure relief. The problem was solved! I now had a reasonable, manageable number of strawberry plants. Yes, I had thrown away several hundred, but I had kept just enough to bear a good crop and produce more plants in future years.

I am a saver by nature. My grandparents helped raise me. They came through the Great Depression and never threw anything away, like many of their peers. I still have second thoughts about getting rid of plastic cottage cheese containers, since my grandma saved hundreds of them! Thankfully recycling is available in our area, so it cuts down on my strange, guilty feelings.

Have you watched the show *Hoarders*? My husband despises it. He says, "It's like a crystal ball view into my future with you." He is a typical guy, happy with zero extras and has, like, one tote of sentimental items in the basement. By contrast, I have QUITE a few more. But I really have cut back after watching *Hoarders*.

If hoarding is a gene, I'm pretty sure I have it. But I can't stand the idea of a future afternoon with a mental-health professional standing in my bathroom, asking an older me, "Can I get you to throw away at least one of these used toothbrushes?" I don't want to put my children through it, and I don't want to face the embarrassment. I have slowly chipped away at my hoard, actually throwing away (not recycling or repurposing) some of the items. That is a big accomplishment for me.

Maybe hoarding isn't your issue. Maybe you don't have a problem throwing anything away. I kind of admire you for it, for your cleanliness and breezy ways. But you kind of scare me too, because I abhor the idea of something truly useful being thrown away.

For example, I was miffed at my non-keeping husband for a week after he threw away my ear buds. Never used, still pristine in their Apple packaging. Why throw away something we could give to someone else or use in the future? His viewpoint: They have been taking up valuable real estate in our junk cabinet for too long. Since then I have learned to straighten up my stuff a bit (or hide it) before I leave town so he doesn't make a clean sweep.

Why does the Bible give us this ultra-practical verse? I think it's because God knew the keepers would keep too much, and the casters would throw away too much. We all need to strike a balance.

I loved reading Jen Hatmaker's hilarious book *7: An Experimental Mutiny Against Excess*, because it taught me I have far too many items of clothing in my closet, far too many trinkets in storage, and far too much food sitting in my pantry. Once or twice per year I can financially and emotionally afford to go through my hoard and give away what I'm not using so I can bless someone else.

I think that's another reason this verse is in the Bible. It teaches us to retain the right amount so we can be generous with our abundance. It teaches us to trust God to give us what we need, to depend on him for our daily provision. He has always blessed me with more than I could hold, and I need to let go more often so others can benefit.

As much as I enjoy the cozy, safe feeling my hoard brings me, I must be honest and say the freedom and relief I experienced after mowing down perfectly good strawberries feels even better. I wasn't designed to carry so much stuff around, and neither were you. Stuff steals our attention away from God. It attracts us because we can feel it, taste it, see it, listen to it, and smell it. We know it's real. Stuff becomes a subtle, sneaky idol. Even old, worn out stuff like cottage cheese containers can turn into an idol of self-sufficiency. All of it says: *God, I don't really need you.*

That's a message I don't want to send.

What I want to do is receive God's blessings like manna. Enough for one day at a time. If I don't accept it, I go hungry. If I hold onto it like a hoard, it will rot.

This dependent stance flies in the face of our materialistic culture. I want to trust God to provide for my needs rather than trusting in my stuff to give me comfort. I want to be okay with keeping what's important and giving away or throwing away what isn't. I want to hold things lightly so I don't get too attached to this world and not buy too much to get me back into future *Hoarders* mode.

The little girl inside is protesting as I write these words. She is worried I will throw away those old treasures in basement totes. I have room for a few. But I won't add more than I need. I have enough love now, out in the wide open. I have proof in nail-pierced hands and feet. I don't need to hide it in a box or a stack anymore. I have more than enough to share.

Prayer:

Heavenly Father,
I confess to you I keep too much. I confess my hidden desire to do without you. Cleanse me of my desire to not throw away enough junk. If I cling to anything, Lord, let it be your presence and your word. Help me remember I'm just passing through this world with its temporal pleasures, and you have much greater treasures stored up for me in heaven.
In Jesus' name, Amen.

Questions for Study and Reflection:

Skim Genesis 3:1-7. What was the underlying reason Adam and Eve chose to eat the forbidden fruit?

When did you hold on to something too long?

When did you feel better after throwing something away?

Have you ever thrown away something you should have kept? How did you feel about it afterward?

Read Matthew 6:19-20. What kind of treasures wait for you in heaven?

Chapter 12: Tearing and Mending

A time to tear and a time to mend.
Ecclesiastes 3:7

When I was learning to sew, I quickly discovered I needed a tool called a seam ripper almost as often as a needle. The seam ripper made quick work of tearing out upside-down sleeves, sewn-in wrinkles, and wonky pleats. I had to tear out the bad seam before I used the needle to mend.

Not everyone sews, but everyone has seasons of tearing and mending relationships. Seasons of tearing a difficult relationship in two. Seasons of mending old damage and piecing hearts back together again.

The Bible holds many stories of torn and mended relationships. Jacob and Esau were twin brothers, at war even in the womb. As they came of age Esau foolishly gave up his birthright to Jacob. Jacob had to flee for his life when Esau learned of Jacob's manipulation. Their sibling relationship was torn to pieces.

For many years Jacob built a life in another land. But as he grew older, he had to return to his homeland and pass through Esau's territory. I love the faith on display in Jacob's prayer as he prepared to meet Esau:

"O God of my father Abraham, God of my father Isaac, LORD, you who said to me, 'Go back to your country and your relatives, and I will make you prosper,' I am unworthy of all the kindness and faithfulness you have shown your servant. I had only my staff when I crossed this Jordan, but now I have become two camps. Save me, I pray, from the hand of my brother Esau, for I am afraid he will come and attack me, and also the mothers with their children. But you have said, 'I will surely make you prosper and will make your descendants like the sand of the sea, which cannot be counted.'" Genesis 32:9-12

Jacob praised God and called himself unworthy of God's blessings. Yet he trusted God and claimed the promise God gave him when he first fled. He moved forward in faith during a season of transition.

Jacob prepared gifts to appease Esau. It doesn't seem like he was willing to mend right then. He was more concerned about being attacked. Perhaps he worried his past trickery still stirred Esau's wrath.

The time to meet arrived. Esau approached with his four hundred men. Jacob divided his household in protective fashion and bowed low before Esau seven times, in a gesture of deep respect.

But Esau ran to meet Jacob and embraced him; he threw his arms around his neck and kissed him. And they wept. Genesis 33:4

It was both *a time to embrace* and *a time to mend.* I'm glad this story is recorded in the Bible. It teaches us to go to God first when it's time to mend damaged relationships. It teaches us to rest on His promises and faithfulness. This story shows us fears can be calmed, relationships can be restored, and hearts can be sewn back together, all with God's help.

To me the most powerful Bible story of *a time to tear* happened on the day of Jesus' crucifixion. Three of the gospel accounts feature this detail:

It was now about noon, and darkness came over the whole land until three in the afternoon, for the sun stopped shining. And the curtain of the temple was torn in two. Jesus called out with a loud voice, "Father, into your hands I commit my spirit." When he had said this, he breathed his last. Luke 23:44-46

The curtain of the temple separated the Most Holy Place from the Holy Place. The high priest entered the Most Holy Place once per year, on the Day of Atonement, to make a sacrifice for the sins of all the people. No one could enter this area except the high priest. He had to follow many regulations before entering upon risk of death. The Most Holy Place was essentially cut off from God's people, a no-access area.

When Jesus died, the thick, heavy curtain was torn from top to bottom, as Matthew records. Why top to bottom? Because it was God's *time to tear.* He came down to us through Jesus, and made Himself fully accessible through Jesus' once-and-for-all sacrifice.

Have you ever felt like God was far away? That you couldn't approach Him without jumping through hoops or walking on eggshells? That God may strike you down for not being good enough, smart enough, or holy enough? Because the curtain was torn, we don't have to perform any rituals to earn God's favor anymore. We don't have to keep track of how many servant events we attend. We don't need to mentally check off the times we attend church or the donations we send to charities. We don't have to rack up shelves of Bible studies and wear crosses around our necks to prove our commitment to God.

We have full access to unveiled grace through Jesus, and we simply must accept Jesus as Lord and Savior to receive it.

The book of Hebrews paints a beautiful picture of how Jesus is now a high priest on our behalf. I love how these verses speak of the curtain:

We have this hope as an anchor for the soul, firm and secure. It enters the inner sanctuary behind the curtain, where our forerunner, Jesus, has entered on our behalf. He has become a high priest forever. Hebrews 6:19-20

Therefore, brothers and sisters, since we have confidence to enter the Most Holy Place by the blood of Jesus, by a new and living way opened for us through the curtain, that is, his body, and since we have a great priest over the house of God, let us draw near to God with a sincere heart and with the full assurance that faith brings. Hebrews 10:19-22

Because God chose *a time to tear* His own Son, we have hope, confidence, assurance, and faith. Our hearts are mended and reconciled to Him. If you live out your seasons with this knowledge, you will gain the peace, joy, and love your heart seeks, and your trust in God's timing will be strong. And no one will pay attention to your mended seams; they will see the rivers of life running through you instead.

Prayer:

Heavenly Father,
You are the master of tearing and mending. I place all my relationships in your hands. Show me which ones need tearing and which ones need mending. Give me courage and strength to reconcile. Thank you for tearing the curtain so I can have full access to your grace and your presence. Remind me to live in the knowledge I need not earn your favor with good works.
In Jesus' name, Amen.

Questions for Study and Reflection:

When have you seen a relationship mended? What happened to facilitate the mending?

Which of your relationships needs mending? How can you ask God to help you?

Skim Hebrews 9. What part of the system of Old Testament sacrifices intrigues you?

Why is Jesus' sacrifice different from the old way of sacrificing?

Read Hebrews 10:19-25. How does God want you to live now that you are reconciled to him?

Chapter 13: Silence and Speaking

A time to be quiet and a time to speak.
Ecclesiastes 3:7 NLT

What a noisy, rushed, busy culture we all live in today. It's hard to sort out the many messages we receive, and it's difficult to feel heard among the masses. I have a very difficult time keeping up with emails and texts, maintaining connections with friends, and carving out time to visit extended family. I'm not the model to follow, to be sure. But I know *a time to be quiet* is an essential counterbalance to all the hustle.

My quiet time is in the morning, before anyone else is up. I get up before 5:00 a.m. and sip my hot tea while I read my Bible. Then I update my blog, check my messages, and take a quick peek at the weather forecast before my children rise and the day begins its full swing. I treasure this quiet, uninterrupted time to commune with God and focus solely on writing.

Since I work at a school, I am blessed to be home around 3:15 p.m. most weekdays. For years I have established a house rule of afternoon quiet time for everyone. My children have a snack, do their homework, and play outside. I retreat to my bedroom and read, nap, or pray before the rush of evening activity begins. An afternoon quiet hour keeps this introvert sane and happy.

On the days I miss out on morning quiet time, I am off-kilter the rest of the day. Small irritations seem huge, my words have an edge to them, and I'm not content with anything. Even on mornings I sleep late, I try to squeeze in 10 minutes of quiet time because I'm well aware of the cost of not doing so.

Afternoon quiet times are not always possible due to appointments and errands. I know to not take on too much that evening if I can't have down time. It's a good night for takeout or prepackaged dinners. It's a good night to turn in a little early.

When do you have quiet time? If you don't have it regularly, can you try it this week and see if it makes a difference in your level of peace?

This is what the Bible has to say about a time to be quiet or still:

But I have calmed and quieted myself, I am like a weaned child with its mother; like a weaned child I am content. Psalm 131:2

In repentance and rest is your salvation, in quietness and trust is your strength. Isaiah 30:15

Be still, and know that I am God; I will be exalted among the nations, I will be exalted in the earth. Psalm 46:10

Quiet times are ideal for meditating on God's word, recalling His faithfulness to you, thanking and praising Him for what He's doing in your season of life, and considering how you can place your trust in Him for what's ahead.

It's perfectly quiet in my house right now. My children are at their grandparents' home, and my husband is out doing his thing until I finish writing today. I spent the last ten minutes taking a break and watching the finches eat sunflower seed from my feeders. Watching the birds gives me a peaceful sense of God's provision. If He faithfully provides for wild birds, surely He is faithfully providing for me (Matthew 6:26).

I held the Bedside Reminder Card page from my last Bible study in my hands and meditated on those scriptures. This one jumped out to me as my theme verse for 2017:

You will keep in perfect peace those whose minds are steadfast, because they trust in you. Isaiah 26:3

I left that quiet ten minutes with a fresh sense of God's presence and a renewed trust in Him for the coming year. In only ten quiet minutes I experienced newness of life. I know God will give you newness of life if you give Him ten exclusive minutes today!

Being quiet comes rather easily to me, and *a time to speak* can be difficult. I have struggled with passivity for most of my life. Not speaking up when I should have, not accepting invitations, not calling friends, not being brave. Letting others speak for me when I was old enough and capable enough to speak myself. The passive life cost me much, and I have worked hard to become more assertive.

I learned to be assertive by standing up to the controlling people in my past. When I confessed my fear of speaking up to my counselor, he said, "I can't guarantee even by saying the right thing in the right way at the right time, anything will change for the better. But I can guarantee if you don't speak up, nothing will change." His comment sunk deep. I sensed it was *a time to speak* if I wanted toxic patterns to change. I will talk more about this in Chapter 15. For now, I'll say none of my relationships changed for the better without my speaking up.

We live in a culture when everyone feels they have a right to vent any opinion at any time they please. Social media makes it tempting and way too easy. If you want to be wise about *a time to speak,* you must trust in God's timing first. Before firing off an email. Before making a snarky comment. Before gossiping behind the offender's back. Pray God will give you his words, not your own. Pray He will grant you the courage to speak up at the right time, or the wisdom to be quiet.

Queen Esther was a Jew, but the king was unaware. Due to a wicked decree her people were set for destruction. Her cousin and advisor Mordecai urged her to speak up and defend her people to the king. He pleaded with her,

"For if you remain silent at this time, relief and deliverance for the Jews will arise from another place, but you and your father's family will perish. And who knows but that you have come to your royal position for such a time as this?" Esther 4:14

Esther fasted and prayed, and decided to approach the king. Her wise timing and intuition saved her people from disaster. Esther's successful campaign depended on her willingness to speak up.

Who needs your speaking up to spare them from harm? Is there anyone in your life who needs an advocate, advisor, or mediator? In this noisy time, this rushed season, hurting people are often overlooked and marginalized. How can your *time to speak* help them today?

Prayer:

Heavenly Father,
I praise you for creating quiet spaces in my life to enjoy only with you. Call me to your side in those quiet moments and still my worries, fears, and doubts. Multiply my trust in you as I spend more time in your word. Lord, help me discern between the times I need to be quiet and the times I need to speak up. Make me wise to your ways and your plans. Reveal to me who I can serve as an advocate, advisor, or mediator.
In Jesus' name, Amen.

Questions for Study and Reflection:

Are you naturally outspoken or quiet? What are the positives and negatives?

If you have ten minutes to spend alone with God today, how will you use it?

Review the three verses on being quiet or still. Which one means the most to you, and why?

Have you ever posted something you later regretted on social media or email? What did you learn from that experience?

Who has served as your advocate, advisor, or mentor? How can you follow their example to help someone else?

Chapter 14: Loving and Hating

A time to love and a time to hate.
Ecclesiastes 3:8

Does it annoy you, as it does me, when retailers stock shelves with two holidays at once? Recently I made a quick stop in a box store a few days before Christmas. Valentine's Day candy was already sitting on the same shelf with Christmas goodies. I don't want to think about Valentine's Day before Christmas! I want to enjoy Christmas and every other holiday in its rightful time and place without any competing seasons edging it out.

Enough of my rant. Seeing those hearts so early made me think: Do we really need retailers to remind us it's *a time to love*? Isn't love something we can do every day without having to think about it?

I know the truth: love can be hard, day in and day out. Love is not always pleasant, wrapped up pretty in pink and lace. Love is surprisingly easy to forget, because we are all selfish creatures.

Every once in a while, I perform a self-test with the love chapter in 1 Corinthians 13:4-8 NLT, to see how true I am to God's standard of love, inserting my name where "love" should be. Fill your name in these blanks:

__________ is patient.
__________ is kind.
__________ is not jealous.
__________ is not boastful.
__________ is not proud.
__________ is not rude.
__________ does not demand his/her own way.
__________ is not irritable.
__________ keeps no record of being wronged.
__________ does not rejoice about injustice.
__________ rejoices whenever the truth wins out.
__________ never gives up.
__________ never loses faith.
__________ is always hopeful.
__________ endures through every circumstance.

This list is humbling. But instead of becoming discouraged, I focus on the areas where I need the most improvement and pray God will help me grow in love.

The area I consistently struggle with most is keeping records of wrongs. This knowledge tells me to focus on forgiving and moving out of the past. Which area is easiest for you? Which area needs more work?

Love is really difficult when someone doles out the opposite of this list to you. Right now, I know someone who delights in injustice and does not rejoice when the truth wins out, when it involves me. This person feels like a thorn in my side. I frequently remember Jesus' words:

But I tell you, love your enemies and pray for those who persecute you. Matthew 5:44

I keep praying for this person to know the love and grace of Jesus. My enemy has several broken relationships and life struggles. I know this person acts in unloving ways toward me because they aren't at peace within. Being loving toward this person is super difficult, but I want to honor Jesus and his clear call to me. Whether I choose it or not, this is my *time to love.*

When this season is past, I want to be proud I "endured through every circumstance" and "never lost faith." I trust something good will come out of this time when love isn't easy.

Hating can be too easy. We live in a culture of hatred. People split into factions and few of us make efforts to understand different perspectives. Sometimes hate feels safer than love. Hatred is running rampant—simply watch the news and you'll see hatred on display all around the world. That's why being brave enough to seize *a time to love* can be a spectacular way of witnessing to a hurting, messed-up world.

However, *a time to hate* what really *needs* to be hated is pretty difficult. This goes back to our discussion about idols in Chapter 8, when you need to "hate" something which isn't good for you.

When my children say they hate something, I tell them, "Hating is a form of breaking the fifth commandment, 'Do not kill.' Hating is so strong, it's like wishing someone were dead. Is that really how you feel?" My children have been schooled every year since kindergarten on following the commandments. They are learning to choose different words from "hate" when they feel frustrated or angry. And so am I!

What attitudes do I wish were dead in my life, but I feed as if I want them to stay alive? My grudges. My tendency to criticize. My hypersensitivity. My excuses. My indulgences. Yuck! (Thanks for allowing me to be honest here.) I need to take a hard look at where those attitudes lead to learn why I need *a time to hate* them. Holding grudges makes me bitter. Criticizing makes me haughty. Overreacting makes me high-maintenance. Making up excuses makes me untrustworthy. Indulging makes me petty.

I don't want to be known for those ugly attitudes. I want to be known to both God and others as someone who does a pretty good job of filling out the blanks in the love chapter with honesty and truth. Not perfect, but getting better at it every day. I want to be known as someone who loves when it's hard and hates when it's harder.

Someone who loves freely, abundantly, and graciously.

Someone who hates injustice and isn't afraid to do something about it.

Someone who inspires others to love like Jesus did.

Prayer:

Heavenly Father,
Nothing can separate us from your love, and for that I thank you. (Romans 8:38-39) Loving can be easy when people love us back, but it's so hard when they don't, Lord. Help me to follow your command to love my enemies. Show me practical ways I can do that. I know there are pockets of hatred in my heart, Father. Weed them out and heal them with your love. Reveal to me which of my attitudes need to be hated, so I can grow to be more Christ-like.
In Jesus' name, Amen.

Questions for Study and Reflection:

How can you use your "easy" area on the love list to bless others this week?

What practical steps can you take to become more loving in your "challenge" area this week?

Read John 12:25. What do you think Jesus intended with the words "love" and "hate" in this verse?

Look up John 13:34-35. Why is loving one another so important?

Read John 15:18-25. How do these verses challenge you? How do they bring you comfort?

Chapter 15: War and Peace

A time for war and a time for peace.
Ecclesiastes 3:8

Watching the television show *Intervention* is one of my guilty pleasures. People who have become slaves to addiction have one final chance to reconcile with family members, who are usually worried the addict will die any day from an overdose.

The show's producers tell the addict they are creating a show about addiction, which is partly true. Meanwhile counselors meet with family members, preparing them for an emotional showdown called an intervention.

The addict is led to a meeting place and is either shocked or angry to see many family members gathered together. I imagine they feel ambushed. The family members each read letters of memories, sadness, pain, love, and ultimatums. They all say, "If you don't enter rehab now, we will cut off all contact with you."

This scene is the height of the battle. The addict faces a difficult choice: suffer through detox and give up a familiar lifestyle, or lose out on their oldest relational ties.

Most addicts choose rehab. Only a few times have I seen an episode where the addict isn't willing to try and isn't moved by the heart-wrenching cries of their loved ones. After watching this show for years, I estimate perhaps half of the addicts sober up after rehab and live clean lives. The other half fall right back into addiction.

I always wonder how those families feel when the addict slips back into addiction, after all the drama. Do they feel like the fight was worthwhile? Do they feel like *a time for war* resulted in *a time for peace*?

I am certain this show intrigues me because I've had many experiences with addicts. Maybe not addicts on the very brink of disaster, but addicts all the same. And if I didn't care about them, I wouldn't keep watching a show about confronting addiction.

Alcoholism is in my DNA. It's a code I don't dare unlock. I purposely limit my drinking to keep from becoming familiar with that dark, destructive side. I know it all too well in the lives of people I love with all my heart. I don't want to join the ranks.

I knew this would probably be the hardest chapter for me to write. Dare I be so honest? Yet, I know many people who never speak of it, but wonder if today is the day to initiate a battle. If today is the day to address the issue that's always present but never discussed. If today is the day to confront after years of silence and denial. If today is *a time for war.*

Beside the Bible, no other book besides *Boundaries* has transformed me more. I drank this book in after alcoholism struck a sudden blow in my family. This book opened my eyes to the many ways I had served as an enabler. It opened my eyes to this truth: God didn't want me to be a people-pleaser anymore, but a boundary-setter.

I waged war by speaking up for myself. I waged war by saying no for the first time in my life. I waged war by setting limits, enforcing consequences, and standing firm. That twenty-something me found newness of life. Freedom. Relief.

A time for war equals pain. You can't have war without fighting, damage, and wounds. None of my hurts were physical, but the emotional counterattacks sent me straight to the counselor's office.

Why did I wage war? Why did I spend years in therapy? I was in pursuit of peace. Even though I had a difficult childhood and a difficult marriage, I never gave up hope that peace was possible. I saw it in other families. I saw it in church. I wanted it for myself. I created *a time for war* in hopes that *a time for peace* was on the other side.

I deeply value peace. I am calm and conflict-averse by nature. I wrote the book *Christmas Peace for Busy Moms* this year, because until 2016, I can't ever remember having a peaceful Christmas. But I realized peace was not going to happen without a fight. My children wouldn't grow up in a peaceful home unless I first went to battle.

I won, only with God's help. Peace reigns now. Peace is possible through boundaries. Stones set up to say, "This far and no further."

I set up encouragement for myself too. Signs which say:

Be strong and courageous. Do not be afraid; do not be discouraged, for the LORD your God will be with you wherever you go. Joshua 1:9

So do not fear, for I am with you; do not be dismayed, for I am your God. I will strengthen you and help you; I will uphold you with my righteous right hand. Isaiah 41:10

They must turn from evil and do good; they must seek peace and pursue it. 1 Peter 3:11

Peacemakers who sow in peace reap a harvest of righteousness. James 3:18

I am no longer too afraid to wage war if it needs to be fought. I found newness of life when I took confidence in the Lord, actively seeking and pursuing peace.

Prayer:

Heavenly Father,
My secret struggles are not hidden from you. You are well aware of the battles I've fought and the reasons why I keep seeking peace. Help me choose only battles worth fighting. Show me when it's time for war in the name of peace. Help me empower and inspire others who have battles to fight and aren't sure how to begin.
In Jesus' name, Amen.

Questions for Study and Reflection:

How has addiction touched your life? How has the struggle drawn you closer to God?

What wars have you waged in the past?

What is your motivation for pursuing peace?

Using a concordance or online Bible search, look up verses on peace. Which verse do you find most meaningful, and why?

Read Psalm 85:10. Why do these two pairs make sense to you?

Chapter 16: Appointed Times

A time for every activity under heaven.
Ecclesiastes 3:1 NLT

So many seasons, so many times, so many activities. We have looked at how God uses each season to give us newness of life.

As I reviewed the chapters, I noticed how much time I spent writing about the negative seasons as compared to the positive seasons. More about grieving than dancing. More about tearing down than building up. I believe God has more lessons in store during hard times. That's been true in my own life of faith. The times I've grown most have been times of struggle and times of waiting.

In my scripture reading today, I came across this verse about Jesus:

A shoot will come up from the stump of Jesse;
from his roots a Branch will bear fruit. Isaiah 11:1

I considered how long the season lasted between Isaiah's prophecy and Jesus' birth. The people who heard Isaiah's message had no idea the shoot would wait inside that stump for hundreds of years.

Newness of life rose from that stump all the same, in God's perfect timing. He planted the seed of new life in the Garden of Eden (Genesis 3:15) and it bore fruit about 2,000 years ago when Jesus was born as the Savior of the world, the Branch in Isaiah's prophecy.

Jesus said this regarding his followers:

I have come that they may have life, and have it to the full. John 10:10

Jesus came that you may have newness of life in all its fullness.

In your seasons of birth and death, Jesus remembers you.

In your seasons of planting and harvesting, Jesus bears fruit through you.

In your seasons of killing and healing, Jesus transforms you.

In your seasons of tearing down and building up, Jesus is your cornerstone.

In your seasons of crying and laughing, Jesus strengthens you.

In your seasons of grieving and dancing, Jesus moves with you.

In your seasons of scattering and gathering, Jesus is faithful.

In your seasons of embracing and turning away, Jesus befriends you.

In your seasons of searching and stopping, Jesus holds you.

In your seasons of keeping and throwing away, Jesus guides you.

In your seasons of tearing and mending, Jesus comforts you.

In your seasons of silence and speaking, Jesus encourages you.

In your seasons of loving and hating, Jesus purifies you.

In your seasons of war and peace, Jesus empowers you.

Will you praise him today as your source of new life in every season?

Prayer:

Heavenly Father,
Thank you for walking by my side in every past season, every current season, and every future season. All my activities belong to you. All my times are in your hand. I trust you to guide me along the path of righteousness for your name's sake. (Psalm 23:3)
In Jesus' name, Amen.

Questions for Study and Reflection:

Read Psalm 16:11. How can you praise God for the path you are on today?

How is God bringing newness of life from a stump in your world?

Do you agree you have learned more from negative seasons than positive seasons? Why or why not?

When you look at the list of what Jesus does in your seasons, which one resonates with you today?

How has this book helped you trust in God? With whom can you share what you've learned?

In Closing

May the God of hope fill you with all joy and peace as you trust in him, so that you may overflow with hope by the power of the Holy Spirit.

Romans 15:13

I hope this study has blessed you in a new way. I would love to hear how God has worked in your heart through this study. Please join my Facebook page at **facebook.com/sarahgeringercreates** and let me know how God is bringing you newness of life. I look forward to reading your comments!

As a thank you gift for joining me on this journey, I want to give you access to special extra resources for this book. Sign up to receive several free goodies at **sarahgeringer.com**.

If you like this study, you will want to join me more studies in 2017. I will cover various topics of spiritual growth.

I will be honored if you are willing to contribute your stories to my future books. Visit my Contact page on my website to let me know you'd like to contribute and I will be in touch with you.

Your review of *Newness of Life: Trusting God in Times of Transition* on Amazon, Goodreads, and other social media will help others find newness of life in their current seasons. **Please take a few minutes to post an honest and helpful review.** I deeply appreciate your shares as I work to expand my writing ministry.

Suggest this book to a friend or family member who is looking for newness of life in their current season. You never know whose life may be changed by spreading the word.

May God bless you as you seek him this year!

Sarah Geringer

Notes

Chapter 6:

1. https://www.facebook.com/DrHenryCloud/photos/a.489655829570.270913.142718314570/10153443234379571/?type=3&theater
2. http://www.smithsonianmag.com/science-nature/the-microscopic-structures-of-dried-human-tears-180947766/?no-ist
3. http://www.smithsonianmag.com/science-nature/the-microscopic-structures-of-dried-human-tears-180947766/?no-ist
4. http://www.mayoclinic.org/healthy-lifestyle/stress-management/in-depth/stress-relief/art-20044456?pg=2

About the Author

Sarah Geringer is a devoted follower of Jesus, wife, mother of three, and a freelance writer and artist. At the age of 16 she felt called to write after God spoke to her while attending a James Taylor concert. She has blogged since 2010, and regularly posts at **sarahgeringer.com.**

Sarah has always loved Bible study. As a child, she gained a strong foundation of Bible knowledge through Lutheran education. When Sarah became a mother, she found friendship, encouragement, and support through small group Bible study at her church. She believes in personal and group Bible study as a primary pathway of spiritual growth.

Sarah has completed a memoir in free verse, *Heart in a Drawer: My Story as a Child of Divorce*. Her other books include *Christmas Peace for Busy Moms* and *The Fruitful Life.*

Sarah holds a Bachelor of Arts in English from Covenant College and a Bachelor of Fine Arts in graphic design and illustration from Southeast Missouri State University. She enjoys reading, drawing and painting, gardening, baking, scrapbooking, journaling, and walking in God's beautiful creation.

Sarah lives with her husband and three children in her beloved home state of Missouri.

Connect with Sarah on her blog and through these other online outlets:
Facebook: **facebook.com/sarahgeringercreates**
Goodreads: **goodreads.com/sarah_geringer**
Pinterest: **pinterest.com/s105**
Twitter: **@sarahgeringer**

Made in the USA
Columbia, SC
12 March 2021